THE CHANGING F.

EXETER

A church had originally been built adjacent to South Gate. Holy Trinity Church is recorded from as early as the twelfth century. Probably rebuilt in the fifteenth century, it was removed with South Gate in 1819. This lithograph, dated 1850, shows the view from inside the city, looking out.

THE CHANGING FACE OF
EXETER

PETER THOMAS

ALAN SUTTON PUBLISHING LIMITED

Alan Sutton Publishing Limited
Phoenix Mill · Far Thrupp · Stroud
Gloucestershire · GL5 2BU

First published 1995

British Library Cataloguing in Publication Data.
A catalogue record for this book is available from the British Library.

ISBN 0-7509-0902-1

Typeset in 12/15 Perpetua.
Typesetting and origination by
Alan Sutton Publishing Limited.
Printed in Great Britain by
Hartnolls, Bodmin, Cornwall.

In medieval times one of the most unusual housing sites was on Exe Bridge. The medieval arched bridge had a number of houses, supported by wooden struts, running along most of its length. Properties often had balconies overlooking the river and steps leading down to it, from where the residents would collect water.

Contents

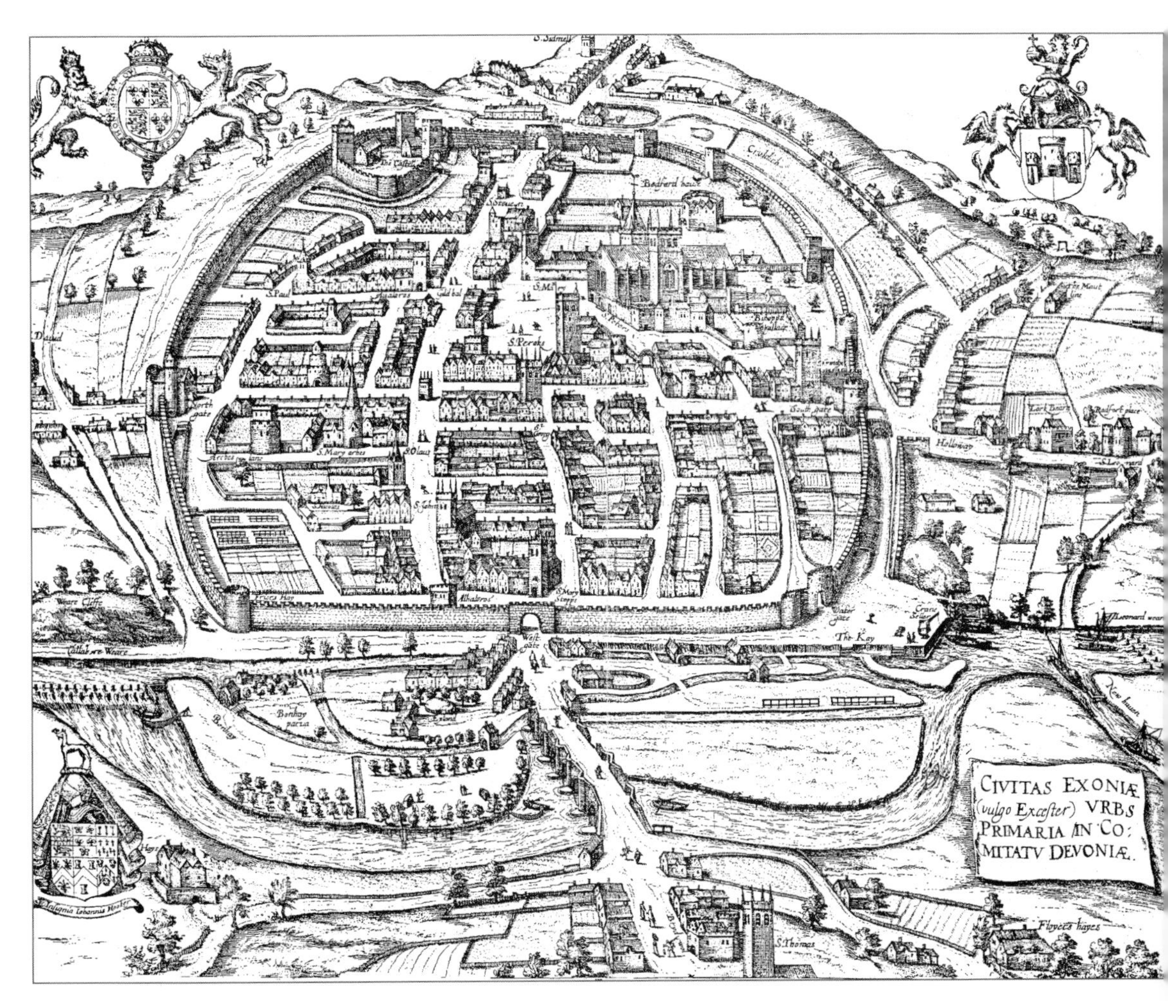

'Exeter in 1618', from Braun and Hogenberg's *Civitates Orbis Terrarum*. This fine early map provides an excellent basis for understanding more about the layout of Exeter at this time. In the foreground, fishermen are netting salmon in the River Exe. Entry to the city from the west is across the medieval Exe Bridge and through West Gate. Ancient leats are shown powering mills in the riverside areas. The city wall, which was constructed in about AD 200 by the Romans, still encloses Exeter. The gates shown – East Gate, North Gate, South Gate and West Gate – are medieval replacements for the earlier Roman structures. Access to the quay is through the Water Gate. This area was to be substantially changed at a later period. In the north-east corner of the city is the castle, created by a curtain wall within the north angle of the city wall at its highest point.

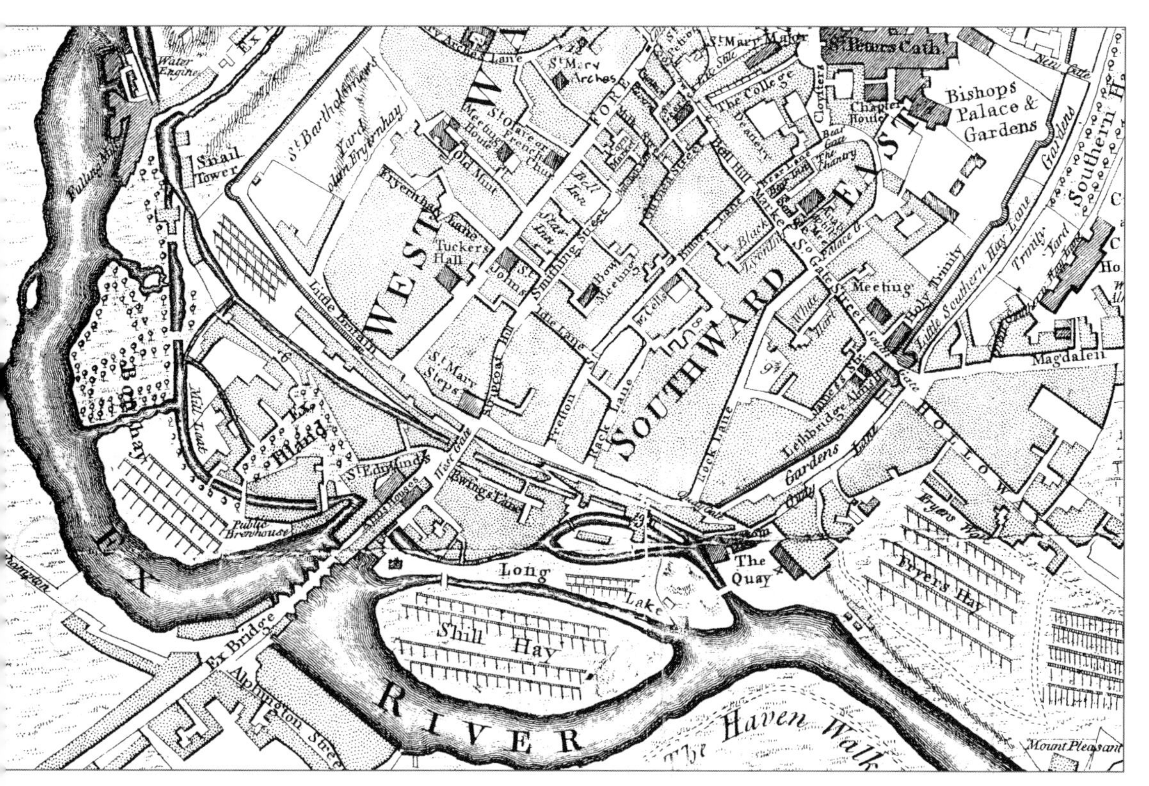

A later map by Benjamin Donn shows the city in 1765. Extensive areas around the city have been given over to the woollen cloth trade. In open fields there are lines of wooden racks, which were used for drying cloth. These were constructed with dozens of hooks to secure the cloth, known as 'tenter hooks'. This is the origin of the saying 'living on tenter hooks'. The woollen cloth trade was to bring wealth to the city from the fifteenth to eighteenth centuries. Places used as rack fields included Snayle Tower, Bonhay, Shilhay, The Fryers, Bull Meadow and a small area near Danes Castle.

ACKNOWLEDGEMENTS

I should like to express my thanks to the Dean and Chapter of Exeter Cathedral for allowing me access to the Cathedral archives and the Cathedral library. In particular I should like to thank the librarian, Peter Thomas, and Angela Doubty, Cathedral archivist, for their help.

My thanks also go to the Devon and Exeter Institution and librarians, Mrs Sheila Stirling and Susan Conniff, for their support and making facilities available to me. I am most grateful. At the Devon County Library Services, West Country Studies, I should like to express my sincere thanks to Mr Ian Maxstead and his staff, without whose help this project would have been difficult to achieve. I am most grateful to the artist, Miss Primrose Pitman, who so kindly allowed me use of her work.

My gratitude is also expressed to Mr Robert Sweetland who drew my attention to items of interest. For use of a fascinating record I am obliged to the Nelson-Atkins Museum of Art, Kansas City, USA. To the many people in Exeter, who over the years have been kind enough to allow me use of their private material, I am indebted, and I hope this publication will add further light on the background of your city.

Lastly, to friend and colleague Lorna, I am especially grateful for the time given in checking texts and for her continuing help and enthusiasm. The project would have been so much more difficult without your help.

INTRODUCTION

This book of images is based on aspects of Exeter which have now disappeared or have radically changed. To illustrate these changes, numerous types of resources have been used, that is etchings, drawings, paintings, maps and photographs. Some of them have never been published before. The work of past artists and photographers have left a valuable resource. Used as single records their importance may not be truly appreciated, but used in context as part of a wider interpretation such pictures can prove invaluable and can add to our understanding of Exeter's past.

Exeter, as one of England's leading historical cities, is a fascinating example of how history and its value is often overlooked or abused. The sweeping away of old buildings and sites has not given Exeter a good reputation for the preservation of its character. It is hard to get away from the word 'demolition' when you are referring to the city's past. Many of those who come to Exeter are often amazed at its lack of foresight in recent times in removing many fine properties.

There are, of course, many reasons for Exeter's destruction, but in order to investigate them we will be concentrating on visual records. The earliest of these dates from around 1700. The maps are older and are somewhat crude by comparison with later examples. The best early example is the Braun and Hogenberg map of 1618. Much of the work shown here relates to the early nineteenth century, when painting, drawing, engraving and etching were becoming more common. From 1880, photographs are more in evidence. Although photography was invented in 1826, the earliest photographic records are unlikely to pre-date 1860, before which time landscape and outdoor studies were very rare, interior and portrait photography being more in vogue.

Over the last 300 years there have been many factors which have effected changes in Exeter. One of the most important was the Turnpike Act of 1753, which led to an unprecedented change to the standard of roads in the area. Major improvements took place over a period of 130 years which were to radically affect Exeter, opening it up for greater use by traffic. During this period the city gates were removed, starting with the North Gate in 1769. By 1820 all of them had been demolished. In 1770 the city opened a new Exe Bridge, the medieval bridge being partially demolished. New Bridge Street was constructed to join the bridge, which involved breaching the city wall. In 1834 the

Iron Bridge was built, spanning the Longbrook Valley, which was made possible by the removal of North Gate.

Queen Street was to be created in 1835, piercing the heart of the city. Its construction also involved the removal of properties, but numerous new buildings were to be built to complement the townscape.

The arrival of the railway in 1844 at St David's brought in a new era. In 1860 trains started to operate from Queen Street, effectively destroying the rural Longbrook Valley, which extended round the north side of the city. The valley was a popular walkway with local residents.

Industrial development was to increase in the riverside areas at this period, and more houses were to be built as a result of an increasing population. In 1905 the introduction of the electric tram involved a number of changes in the city, including the demolition of buildings from South Street up High Street, which opened up St Petrock's Church. A single-span iron bridge replacing the earlier stone structure was opened in 1905 by Mayor C. Perry. The era of four-wheeled traffic had arrived and the horse was to disappear from Exeter's streets.

In the 1930s, major clearance schemes relocated many of Exeter's citizens into new housing estates, with demolition removing a number of interesting ancient buildings in the West Quarter. The most significant event to affect Exeter was the Second World War. A major raid in May 1942 destroyed one third of the central area of the city in just seventy-four minutes, the local authority then demolishing every remaining standing building. The result was an extraordinary view across a devastated city. Post-war redevelopment saw the city destroy much of its remaining historical character. The new style adopted for the design of the city centre took little account of its past and resulted in an unimaginative and monotonous design. In the past fifteen years the city has made strides to rectify some of its past errors, but of course in many respects it is too late.

The period between the mid-1950s and the 1980s was a time when it appeared that anything 'old' had to go, and this was achieved with determination and gusto. It was a sad indictment for such a historical city that it should have so undervalued its past. The conservation of old buildings is often an emotive issue, but Exeter has seen fit to remove properties of great merit and in some cases of national importance. The integration of such properties was, it appears, rarely considered. Instead, only total demolition of whole areas sufficed.

We are fortunate to have resource centres that have retained many records of the city's past. Together with examples from my own private collection, I hope that this material will give the reader an insight into one of England's great historical 'lost' cities.

Peter Thomas
Exeter 1995

CHAPTER ONE

THE CITY WALL AND GATES

Perkin Warbeck attacked East Gate and North Gate on 17 and 18 September 1497. The citizens staunchly defended the city, with the result that more than 400 men from Warbeck's army were killed. Henry VII thanked the people of Exeter by giving his sword and cap of maintenance to the city. These can still be seen in the Guildhall.

Largest of all the gates, East Gate defended the side of the city most vulnerable to attack. The natural defences of Exeter – steep slopes on the north and south sides – acted as deterrents against invasion, but land to the east was reasonably flat and allowed an easier approach. East Gate was therefore a very substantial structure consisting of two drum towers with a central entrance passage. Above the entrance in an alcove stood a statue of Henry VII, which was placed there in 1516. East Gate was demolished in 1784.

West Gate lacked the grandeur and fortification of East Gate and was described as 'a mean structure', having little of architectural interest. The simple entrance faced the traveller who had crossed the medieval Exe Bridge from the west. A porter's lodge was integrated into St Mary Steps Church and can be seen through the entrance at the base of Stepcote Hill. The porter took tolls from travellers. West Gate was demolished in 1815.

North Gate was approached by a steep incline from the Longbrook Valley. Entry into the city proved to be one of the most difficult owing to the gradient. Despite the road level being raised it still proved unsatisfactory, with the final solution being the building of the Iron Bridge in 1834. North Gate was demolished in 1769.

North Gate was reconstructed in wood and plaster for the Diamond Jubilee of Queen Victoria in 1897.

The second largest of the city's gates was South Gate, an imposing structure which was removed in 1819. Properties were often built right up against the gates. The entrance to Little Southernhay is on the right.

This second gate was recreated for Queen Victoria's Diamond Jubilee in 1897. South Gate, however, was not to be placed on its original site: it is shown re-erected adjacent to the White Hart Hotel in South Street.

South Gate was an appalling prison for felons and debtors. The prisoners were kept in cells under which an open sewer flowed. They were occasionally given the opportunity to gain fresh air from an upper storey room. From here they were allowed to beg for alms by hanging their shoe on a string from the window down into the street. The room was known as the Shoe Room and gave rise to the expression 'living on a shoestring'.

'Henry VII at East Gate, 1497', from a painting by G.G. Palmer.

In 1549 West Gate came under siege during the Prayer Book Rebellion. Rebels tried to undermine the city wall and blow it up. Their efforts were detected by a miner, with the result that citizens flooded the passages using domestic water, thereby saving the city.

Perkin Warbeck stormed and burnt North Gate in 1497, but again the citizens repulsed the attack.

The surrender to the Parliamentarians at South Gate, 13 April 1646.

A later etching of 1834 by John Gendall shows South Gate after the demolition of Holy Trinity Church. The gate was also later removed.

This reproduction from an unsigned watercolour shows for the first time another of the Cathedral precinct gates – Bear Gate. The top of Palace Gate is at the junction with Bear Street, which still leads to South Street. The open area in the foreground was known as Deanery Square. On the corner of the street is Selwoods Cottage, an intriguing building dated 1707 of which little is known. Behind it, Bear Gate spans Bear Street. The huge wooden gates are pushed back against the wall. Accommodation is provided above the gates in a long gabled corridor, which could have housed a porter. The gates were locked at night at the ringing of the curfew bell.

The murder of Cathedral official (Precentor) Walter Lechlade in 1283 was to lead to the enclosure of the Cathedral precincts for security reasons. Access was given by seven gates, some for wheeled traffic and some for pedestrian use. The most prominent of them was Broad Gate, which led from the High Street to Cathedral Yard. It provided the processional way to the Cathedral. A porter was responsible for the opening and closing of the gates. Broad Gate was demolished in 1825.

Exeter's Roman city wall, constructed in about AD 200, is one of the city's most historical features and a national monument. An extraordinary decision was made in the 1960s to remove a section of the wall to create Western Way. In the immediate post-war period another extensive portion was demolished to create the top of Princesshay. This section was marked by a line of crazy paving to show its original position. Such actions led to Exeter adding to its reputation for the destruction of its historical sites and buildings.

Pre-war, many properties had gardens abutting the city wall. It was not possible then to walk all the way round the wall as one can today. Destruction in the Second World War and the removal of many properties afterwards opened up this architectural feature as never before. Here, gardens have been removed behind the terraces in Southernhay in preparation for office extensions and a landscaped walkway in 1975.

St Mary's Chapel stood within Castle Yard, as seen in this engraving of 1831. This ancient chapel had for much of its life been disused. In latter times an armoury was stored in the building. With the demolition of the chapel in 1787, the armoury was disposed of, being either given away or sent for scrap. Some pieces remained under a gallery in one of the courts for a period of time.

A plan from the historian Alexander Jenkins' *The History and Description of the City of Exeter*, published in 1806, shows Rougemont Castle 'as it was in the sixteenth century'. A drawbridge or sally-port is shown extending into Northernhay. No trace of this is now visible. In 1612 Northernhay was levelled and then landscaped. A fine gravel path was laid and benches provided. By this time, the sally-port had become ruinous.

An early engraving showing the ruinous drawbridge projecting from the castle wall. The first planting of trees is on the right. A walkway also existed on top of the castle wall, entry to which was from a flight of steps near East Gate.

CHAPTER TWO

LEATS AND CONDUITS

At a number of places on the leats were 'dipping steps'. These provided access to water for Exeter's citizens. This detail from an illustration in Thomas Shapter's book, *The Cholera Epidemic of 1832*, shows water carriers collecting water. This would be taken to Waterbeer Street (the street of the water sellers or bearers) and sold.

An important site historically is Engine Bridge at the junction of Bonhay Road and Exe Street. Water was diverted here from the River Exe to power the city's mills and supply water. The leat shown here divides into the higher and lower leats, and although still flowing the lower leat is mostly culverted. By the end of the seventeenth century a wooden engine was installed on this site to pump water up into the city to a cistern situated at the rear of the Guildhall. Head Weir Mill, shown on the left, is now known as the Mill on the Exe. It was a paper mill. The Victorian Engine Bridge Cottages have been demolished in recent times.

The site at Engine Bridge, 1832, showing Mount Dinham cliffs and, below, Engine House.

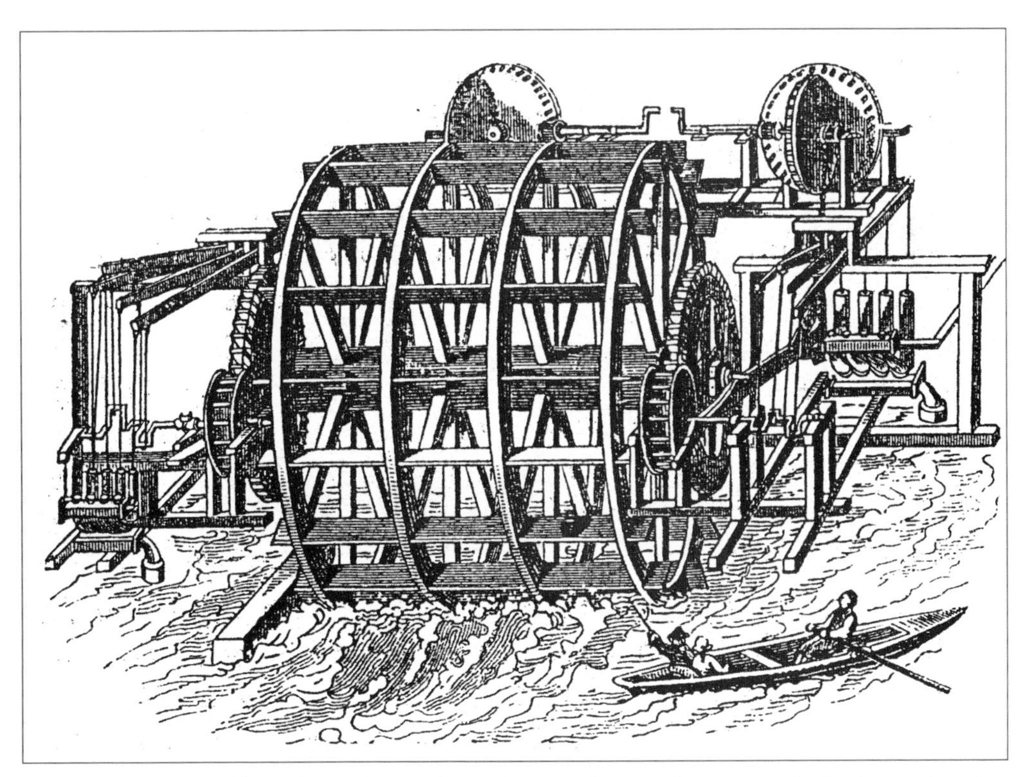

'The water engine at old London Bridge' indicates the type of engine that was installed at Exeter, but of course smaller. The name Engine Bridge is derived from the water engine.

The system of leats in Exeter provided some intriguing views, mostly now lost. Post-war redevelopment removed extensive stretches of open leats that had been familiar for centuries. This photograph of about 1920 shows the lower leat flowing beside Commercial Road after leaving the medieval Exe Bridge at a site known as Horse Pool. The side of Tremletts Tannery is shown on the left and on the right are the backs of cottages. Overhanging the leat and attached to the rear of the cottages are toilets. There was no need for underground sewerage systems.

Cricklepitt Mill is the only mill left in central Exeter and, although semi-derelict, it still has all of its working parts and could be restored. Its fate, however, may lie in the balance. This reproduction from a watercolour shows the mill in working order and is dated *c.* 1830. In the foreground is the small bridge that spanned the lower leat. The leat is now culverted at this point. Should this important historical building and adjacent properties suffer the same fate as many in Exeter, it will be a most sad reflection upon the city.

This photograph from the turn of the century was taken from outside Cricklepitt Mill looking up the higher leat. On the left is the quaint row of cottages named Leat Terrace. Householders display colourful window-boxes and a caged bird enjoys the sun. Exonians would catch eels in the leats, and occasionally prisoners would be brought to clean them out. Compare this view with the photograph shown on p. 66; much has changed.

The provision of fresh water for Exeter can be traced back to the mid-twelfth century, when it was brought from the east of the city. The piped water was made available from conduits, St Peter's Conduit in The Close being the first to be erected. In 1461 the Great Conduit was built at the junction of High Street and South Street. The site was known as the Carfoix (crossroads). This conduit, removed in 1770, was replaced by another, which was built further down South Street, but the site proved to be unsatisfactory. It was demolished in 1799 and rebuilt further down the street. In 1834 it was removed and replaced by a granite conduit in the shape of an obelisk at the end of George's Lane and Milk Street.

The Great Conduit at the Carfoix.

Detail of the South Street Conduit.

The South Street Conduit from a painting by George Townsend, *c.* 1830. Water carriers are shown going about their business. The conduit is outside what appears to be the College of the Vicars Choral in South Street.

The gifted artist, Miss Primrose Pitman, captures a unique historical record. Looking over New Bridge Street, the scene shows the medieval Exe Bridge and St Edmund's Church before partial demolition in the 1970s and, importantly, a background of industrial buildings. Most of these properties no longer exist. Miss Pitman has contributed considerably to the visual records of the city, being a skilled etcher.

One of the most important aspects of Exeter has been its historical link with the River Exe which flows at the foot of the city. For centuries bridges have created a link with the west side of the city; the earliest structures were probably wooden, then stone. The single-span iron bridge shown here in about 1960 was opened in 1905. It provided an elegant entry into the city. Today virtually nothing exists from this scene, all buildings and the bridge itself being demolished in the 1970s. The continuation of the inner bypass to the riverside decimated the area. Today the entry into Exeter from the west is featureless and uninteresting. Two concrete bridges have replaced the fine single-span iron bridge.

Exeter's medieval bridge still exists, but only in part. Of the original eighteen arches, only eight remain. The bridge was built in about AD 1200 under the initiative of Walter Gervase, Mayor. It continued to serve the city until 1770. Today declared a national monument, the remains of the bridge stand on dry land. The identity of the artist who painted this early picture is unknown.

A view from Exe Bridge, dated 1850, shows Shilhay before major industrial development. This area looks distinctly like an island, but the waterways were man-made. At this date, Shilhay is dominated by timber-drying sheds. The leat called Coney Lake is on the left.

A superb lantern slide provides an excellent record of ships at the quay. Such scenes are very evocative of the heyday of Exeter as a port.

'The quay, 1835', drawn from nature by C.F. Williams. At this time the warehouses would have been virtually new, having been built in 1835. It is interesting to note the smoking chimneys and a horse-drawn sledge on the quay. A queue of people appears to be waiting at the Ferryman's Cottage for the ferry boat.

An early aerial view over the quay and city, dated 1828, shows the port very much in decline. By 1970 no further commercial shipping was using Exeter quay. Buildings were in a poor state of repair and little interest was shown in the area. Over the last fifteen years the City Council have instigated a major initiative to revitalize the area. Today nearly all major buildings have been restored and greater emphasis placed on using the area for leisure and recreation. This area has played a major role in the history of Exeter and its importance cannot be overlooked.

A copper engraving of 1823 shows the Knave of Clubs, a large inn that stood near the river at Larkbeare. Entry to the Exeter Ship Canal is in the foreground.

Many old riverside properties have now disappeared. A walk towards Trew's Weir in about 1910 shows a number of houses adjacent to the river. This record is from a lantern slide.

CHAPTER THREE

LANDSCAPES AND VIEWS

A view from Exwick in 1852 shows that a substantial building had been erected – St David's station. The railway first came to Exeter in 1844. The tunnel that was to link St David's station to Queen Street station is shown newly built. Below the two hunters is Exwick Church.

The earliest views of Exeter date from around 1670, as in this south-west view. This resembles more of a flat plan, but still gives a good impression of the city at this time. Shipping is seen in the river and to the right are rack fields. Exeter is seen as a tight and compact area within the city wall. Professor Hoskins, the noted historian, tells us that in the early sixteenth century the population stood at about 8,000 people. The figure today is approximately 106,000.

A romantic view, dated 1828, shows buildings clutching to the west side of the city. Colleton Crescent dominates the scene and beside it rack fields are laid out.

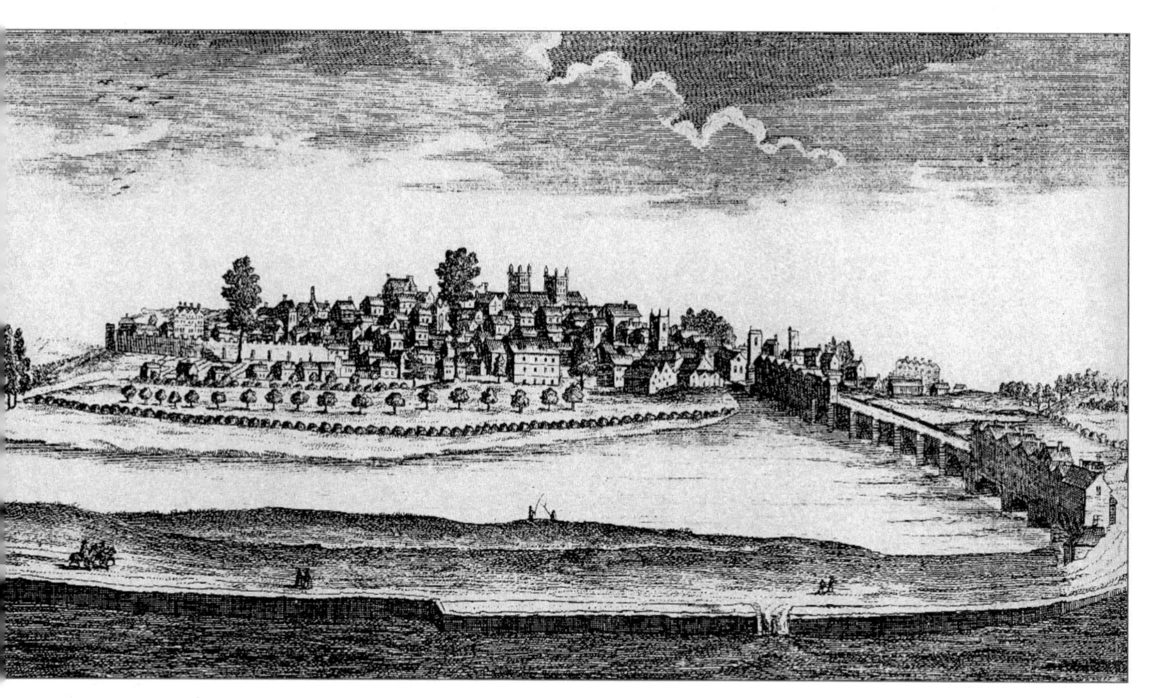

'A prospect of Exeter, 19 August 1723.' The medieval Exe Bridge is seen at its full extent crossing the river. St Edmund's Church is at the end of the bridge, just before entering West Gate. On the northern side of the city is the city wall. At this time there is no indication of any major building on the riverside.

This lithograph by G. Rowe, dated 1828, gives a good impression of entry into the city from Pennsylvania. A wagon and stagecoach are making their way down the hill. The central area is full of mature trees. Southernhay is in front of the Cathedral with a backdrop of the Haldon Hills.

'Exeter from Blackboy Road, 1846' shows some unusual features in the shape of two conical towers. These were brick-drying kilns. The manufacture of bricks still takes place a short distance away in Monks Road, Mount Pleasant. At the top of Blackboy Road was the toll gate and open country.

For citizens today it is difficult to appreciate just how close the countryside came to central Exeter. This view, drawn from nature by C.F. Williams in 1835, looks across open country to the Cathedral and Southernhay. The foreground is basically Barnfield. Here a couple are milking, with barns close by. It is an idyllic scene. Only forty-one years earlier the magnificent Georgian terraces of Southernhay had been created and today they are still one of the city's finest features.

Drawn from nature on stone by W. Spreat Jnr, this view from Union Road near Clifton Place indicates how rural the city was 150 years ago. A couple have been milking and cows idly graze in the fields. A haystack is shown on the right.

The Exe Valley in 1829–32, looking towards Exeter, in a steel engraving by Petit. There is a proliferation of trees, and the 'pepperpot' church of St David's can just be seen to the left of the Cathedral.

The Longbrook Valley to the north of Exeter was one of the city's natural defences. The steep-sided valley provided a natural walkway for residents from the St David's area. A path led to the church, the tower of which is seen in the distance. The House of Correction is on the right. The coming of the railway in 1860 obliterated the valley. This is a steel engraving dating from 1831.

The view from Northernhay, shown in 1832, with the House of Correction or Devon County Bridewell, built in 1809. Adjacent to it is the Devon High Gaol, erected in 1794. This site was clearly isolated from the city.

Trading in the streets of Exeter was common practice before the building of the purpose-built markets – the Lower Market in Fore Street and the Higher Market in Queen Street. All manner of goods were sold from small stalls, as seen on the right of this engraving. Under the Guildhall portico, a popular rendezvous point, there is an open but railed area. Two rooms used by the Mace Sergeants to the left and right of the entrance were transferred for the use of the police in 1836.

The riverside setting of Exeter has always been one of its great assets. Historically, this aspect has been much loved by artists. The River Exe is seen here, in 1831, in a very natural state. Trew's Weir is shown and, high above the river, Colleton Crescent and the Cathedral dominate the skyline.

The Exeter Ship Canal, the oldest pound lock canal in England, was started in 1563. On completion it extended 5¼ miles from Exeter to Turf Lock. Lighters are seen making their way up to the quay.

This attractive drawing of Quay Bridge, by Henry Courtney Selous, dated 9 July 1831, shows to the left an enclosed area with a wooden fence. This was traditionally a coal depot. Buildings in the rear could be timber-drying sheds. The Custom House is on the right. All buildings on the skyline have now been demolished.

Chapter Four

Fore Street to High Street

At the junction of Mary Arches Street and Fore Street a variety of properties were once seen. Elegant street lamps, fine decorative iron work, gilt sign writing, tassled shop blinds and other features added to the interest of the street. The narrow entrance to Mary Arches Street is on the left.

Traditionally, Fore Street has always attracted the city's tradesmen. Entering the city from this street at the turn of the century, the visitor would have seen a variety of trades and much activity. Halfway up the street the bracketed clock (illuminated at night) of St John's Church welcomed all and was a feature of the street. This photograph dates from about 1910.

The top of Fore Street in about 1910 looks very different from today. The Church of St Olave's and the adjacent building remain, but only the ground floor of the latter. Examples of the decorative plaster garlands with a bull's head are still visible on what was a three-storeyed building. The plasterwork was recently restored.

Evans Gadd, wholesale druggists and stationers, is shown in premises at the top of Fore Street. Extensive new buildings were built for this company in Smythen Street. Today they are obsolete and for sale. This photograph of about 1890 shows to the right the Devon and Exeter Coffee Tavern with its overhanging lamp. An outsize coffee pot stands on top of the window. The street at this time contained a number of three-storey buildings.

Nos 78 and 79 Fore Street were a pair of seventeenth-century houses that in latter years became known as the Chevalier Inn. Although they were some of the city's most historical and well-known buildings, they were threatened with demolition in 1929 but thankfully saved by the City Council. They were bombed in 1942. This etching is by Miss Hayman. No. 79 featured a famous ridge tile. These were to be found elsewhere in Devon, but were rare. Unfortunately this fascinating feature was lost.

Equestrian figure as seen on No. 79 Fore Street.

An etching of 1927 by Miss Hayman shows the entrance into Mary Arches Street from High Street. Earlier buildings in this street still existed post-war, but were later demolished. St Mary Arches Church has four decorative balls on the tower. These originally stood on the conduit in South Street.

This fascinating photograph, dating from the 1870s, shows the corner of North Street with High Street. On the corner of North Street is the premises of J. May & Co., ironmonger. A giant lock hangs over the doorway. At this time a number of older premises stood on North Street, which complemented one another. After 1880 little remained of the old street, which was transformed by the building of a substantial property for Messrs Cornish & Co.

This photograph shows the demolition of the corner of High Street and North Street prior to rebuilding in 1880. A large lock above the door advertises the locksmith. Note the horse feeding out of a bucket at the rear of the building.

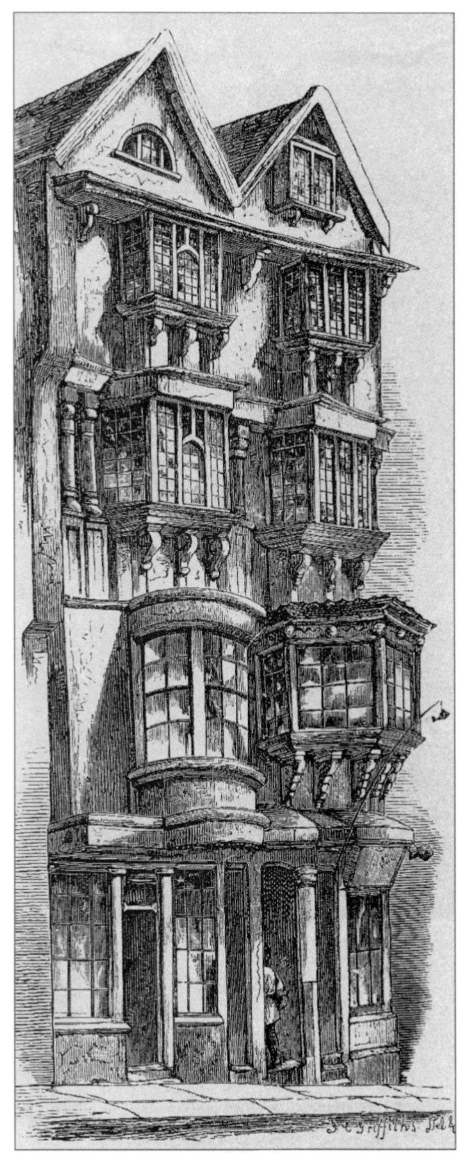

Nos 19 and 20 North Street were of special historical interest but were demolished in 1890. The bow-fronted window was to be removed and integrated into No. 229 High Street, where it may be seen today.

Above: Nos 19 and 20 North Street by Griffiths from the book *An Elizabethan Guild*, published in 1873. Note the fishmonger's sign. *Left*: Lower North Street, *c*. 1890.

North Street appears to have been a more confined street in about 1900, with a small square at its end. A covered wagon advertising John Lock, baker and confectioner, is parked on the site, and the Iron Bridge is in the background.

The junction of High Street and North Street, *c.* 1890. St Peter's Corner was a meeting place for many Exonians, here a little suspicious about having their photograph taken. Above them is the signboard of Holman Ham and Co., druggist, established in 1765.

High Street at the Guildhall, *c.* 1885. A horse-drawn bus passes the Guildhall. These vehicles and horse-drawn trams were to give way to electric trams in 1905.

Numerous small churches were tucked away in Exeter. Some were little used, which led to their removal. On the corner of Goldsmith Street is the tiny church of Allhallows, which was demolished in 1906. The entrance to this street hardly allowed a wagon to pass down it.

Looking from the Guildhall portico, numerous shop blinds, which extended to the pavements' edge, were a feature of High Street. Shoppers could arrive by carriage and take advantage of cover from the sun or rain.

This early drawing by George Townsend gives an indication of the buildings found at the junction of Goldsmith Street and High Street, *c.* 1830.

The central connecting street between High Street and Paul Street – Goldsmith Street – was one of Exeter's most ancient, its origins lost in antiquity. The unimaginative design of the new Guildhall Shopping Centre destroyed this interesting and valuable short cut.

A superb record of a horse-drawn wagon entering Goldsmith Street from High Street. The door of Allhallows' Church is on the right.

Upper High Street from Castle Street, *c.* 1900. The post-war rebuilding of central Exeter from the 1950s onwards dramatically changed the historic feel of the city's High Street. A uniform style of architecture with little detail or interest was a poor substitute for the variety and style of pre-war buildings. To visit Exeter before the war was an experience that would not be forgotten, as centuries of history had shaped the city and created a unique atmosphere. The photograph above gives a good indication of the variety of architecture in Upper High Street at that time.

In 1900 this elegant building extended from Queen Street into High Street. Its proportions and design were well incorporated into the site. Completed in 1849, it was removed in 1968. Its modern replacement (C&A) was to be one of the most contentious issues in Exeter's post-war development. The concerns were to be justified when a building lacking in any sensitivity for its site was erected.

The junction of Queen Street and High Street, *c.* 1910. The premises occupied by Hinton Lake, chemists, and the *Western Times* (Nos 41 and 42 High Street) bore an elaborately carved panel with the date 1564, when the building was constructed. An advert by Hinton Lake states that before 1740 it was known as the Mansion House and used as judges' lodgings, housing the notorious Judge Jeffreys during the Bloody Assizes in 1685. The buildings are now well restored and add to the variety of the street.

One of the most impressive façades in High Street fronted the Commercial Union building, which stood almost opposite St Stephen's Church. Splendidly classical, it was adorned with a figure of King Alfred and was a noted landmark. The well-known jewellers, Bruford, with a timber shopfront, displayed a massive clock supported by 'Old Father Time'.

The view down High Street from the junction with Bedford Street, *c.* 1930.

The Half Moon Hotel on the corner of High Street and Bedford Street was to be removed to make way for the building of Lloyds Bank in 1906. The bank occupied a ground-floor site. Deller's Café was to be integrated into the side and above the bank. Entry to Bedford Circus is beyond the hotel.

This is one of a series of drawings by Baird, and shows High Street, with St Lawrence's Church, which was blitzed and gutted in 1942.

Central High Street with St Lawrence's Church, *c.* 1915. The Empire Cinema is adjacent to the church.

CHAPTER FIVE

SOME SIDE STREETS

Lants Almshouses, a charming row of cottages, extended along the city wall in Bartholomew Street and overlooked the yard of the Crown and Sceptre Hotel. Built in 1763, each house had a half-door, which enabled residents not only to look directly out on the street but also to chat to the next-door neighbour without stepping outside the house. These delightful houses were removed in the 1930s for a proposed road-widening scheme that never transpired.

Leat Terrace took its name directly from the leat that ran in front of it. Providing accommodation for those working in the nearby industries, the little terrace was to be removed in the 1970s with the encroachment of the new Western Way. (See p. 27 for an earlier view of this same scene.)

No. 18 North Street, dating from about 1600, still retains its original covered passageway, which leads to the rear of the premises. This is the only example of a timber-framed passageway left in the city, and it still has its flagstone floor. This etching is by Miss Hayman and shows the rear of the building, looking to North Street.

Catherine Street takes its name from the fifteenth-century almshouses, of which only a ruin exists today. An important backstreet connecting The Close to Bedford Street, Catherine Street contained a number of interesting buildings, which the architect James Crocker illustrated in his book, *Sketches of Old Exeter*, which was published in 1886. This shows a variety of premises with old inns, shops and passageways. Sadly, little is left except for the ruined almshouses and Oddfellows Hall, which was built in 1906.

Bowden Court, one of the city's many pre-war courts, survived until the 1970s, when it was demolished. Its removal was part of the major plan to demolish buildings from the junction of South Street with Magdalen Street, allowing the new Western Way inner bypass to gain access to the river. The scheme was to obliterate this part of the city. The Regency iron gates of Bowden Court can now be seen at the rear of St Nicholas' Priory in Mint Lane, off Fore Street.

Coombe Street in an etching by Miss Hayman of 1927. On the right is the Coombe Street Chapel, later to become a morgue and after the war a night club. A gabled archway opposite is one of the entrances to Central School.

Originally, Coombe Street joined West Street to South Street without interruption. Today, the Western Way truncates the little street, leaving only the former Coombe Street Chapel to recall some of the area's former character.

Before the turn of the century, Paul Street was a small complex of buildings and courtyards. These were gradually removed. The north side, shown here, was to become the bus and coach station, but today is the site of the Harlequin Shopping Centre.

Old Paul Street (north side), reproduced from a Worths postcard.

Paul Street in 1925, with St Paul's Church standing at the head of the street. To the right, immediately in front of the church, is the entrance to Goldsmith Street. A wagon is turning to enter the street. Only a small part of Goldsmith Street now exists, at the junction with High Street.

The south side of Paul Street, showing the entrance to Goldsmith Street before it was destroyed by the construction of the Guildhall Shopping Centre. Today the site consists of a massive brick wall with service entrances, and is of no architectural merit whatsoever.

CHAPTER SIX

THE WEST QUARTER

This photograph was taken at the turn of the century, and shows the barbers, F. Williams, on the corner of West Street. A traditional barber's pole is outside the shop. In the 1930s this property, possibly dating from as early as the sixteenth century, was demolished. The site was to remain empty for thirty-one years.

No other street in Exeter has attracted artists as much as Stepcote Hill. Not only did the steep medieval street have a number of harmonious buildings that created a pleasing townscape, but it also supported a community which was obviously very gregarious. Here we see washing hung out of a window on a stick. These small properties had little or no garden for the drying of clothes.

This etching by John Gendall shows Stepcote Hill, with a wooden walkway over the gutter as it ends in West Street. A small plaque on the bottom property states 'Peter Dunn, General Dealer'. Two chickens search for food outside the front door, and two ladies peep around the corner of Parsonage Lane.

Despite impoverished conditions for some residents in the West Quarter, many couples had numerous children. Stepcote Hill was a natural playground. Here we see a community mother overseeing a large group of children, *c.* 1910.

Repairs take place on the drainpipe on St Mary Steps Church, *c.* 1915. At this time the surface of West Street was made up of granite sets. The timber-framed house was to be restored in the 1930s after a campaign for its retention. Behind this building is a tiny lane, which at one time led to the Parsonage, hence its old name Parsonage Lane.

This view looking down Stepcote Hill after the restoration of the premises shows the mock Tudor Teignmouth Inn at the corner of Ewings Lane.

This photograph, taken in the late 1930s, shows the restored sixteenth-century houses in West Street, as seen from the Teignmouth Inn. This inn was demolished following the construction of the Western Way.

Major slum clearance in the 1930s was to make radical changes to the West Quarter and create the first housing estates at Burnthouse Lane, residents having to be relocated. One of the city's most historical streets, Stepcote Hill, was to be mostly demolished. The design for replacement buildings took little account of the nature of the street, particularly the upper section. This view shows the start of demolition.

Smythen Street, which joined Stepcote Hill, was the street of the butchers and was given the name Butchers Row. In the early nineteenth century, open-fronted shops lined the street. On the ground floor the shopfronts consisted of large wooden flaps dropped during the day to hold meat. Carcasses were hung outside for all to inspect. At night the shop flaps were drawn up, the shopkeeper retiring upstairs. Blood and offal were washed away down the central gutter. Unfortunately, this often came down over Stepcote Hill, much to the annoyance of the local residents. This picture dates from 1831.

No. 15 Frog Street was said to date from the late sixteenth century. It was situated at the north end of Frog Street, overlooked by New Bridge Street. It was of simple construction, being of two storeys, and was possibly the property of an early local tradesman. The building was demolished in 1961.

Preston Street, *c.* 1900, taken from a lantern slide. The narrow turning into Rack Street is on the left. At the junction of Market Street and Sun Street, Preston Street continued to join West Street. It was a short distance from the industrial area and the quay. A number of fine properties had been erected in the street, probably originally owned by wealthy merchants.

The gifted etcher Miss Hayman captures 'Tuder Street as seen from Bonhay Road'. The tower of Allhallows' Church in Bartholomew Yard is in the background. Today the area known as Exe Island has been altered beyond recognition.

This delightful and unusual view shows properties in Exe Street seen from under the Iron Bridge in Lower North Street. None of these dwellings now exists. The area has been subject to extensive redevelopment and is today one of the city's conservation areas. (Etching by Miss Hayman)

CHAPTER SEVEN

INDIVIDUAL BUILDINGS

The property of the Bampfylde family until 1814, Bampfylde House was to have a number of tenants. In 1934 it was to be opened to the public after being purchased by the City Council. The generosity of Councillor Arthur Guest allowed the house to be acquired for the citizens of Exeter. Architect James Crocker produced this fine drawing on 13 January 1885.

Bampfylde House, dating from 1590, was one of Exeter's greatest architectural treasures. It stood at the corner of Bampfylde Street and Catherine Street. This fine building was totally gutted in 1942, and its remains were demolished.

The entrance to Bampfylde House would have been very familiar to Exonians. Originally the whole property was surrounded by a high wall, and had its own courtyard.

The most famous feature of Bampfylde House was The Oak Room, which was decorated with a highly ornate plaster ceiling, carved oak panels, a wooden cornice and a superb chimney-piece. The coat of arms of the Bampfylde family was displayed over the fireplace. The ceiling was a later edition dating from 1720. Amias Bampfylde continued to enrich the property after the death of his father.

The superbly executed coat of arms of the Bampfylde family, hung over the fireplace.

The City Council was to furnish the building with period furniture to complement the splendid interior.

The Elizabethan bedroom featured an unusual plaster ceiling and a fine four-poster bed.

No. 16 Edmund Street, dating from about 1430, is now one of the city's landmarks and is called 'the house that moved'. This unpretentious timber-framed building was to cause major disruption to post-war redevelopment. A preservation order in the 1950s secured the building for future generations. The decision to move the dwelling took ten years to transpire, being the subject of heated debate. This view looks down Frog Street to New Bridge Street.

A new site for the building was designated at West Gate. The house had received some restoration in the 1930s. Some infill can be seen in this photograph.

On 9 December 1961, the property is on the move encased in a timber corset. It was lifted from its site, where it had stood for 500 years, on to a chassis fitted with iron wheels. Rails had been laid and the property attached to a winch. The 100 yard move ran into problems at the Teignmouth Inn, where the building became jammed. Quick work with a saw solved the problem.

The move created worldwide news. Winched at a rate of 40 yards a day, the two-day operation ended a ten-year saga. Ironically, the new site designated for the old building at West Gate was occupied by a property possibly of equal age that had been removed in the 1930s. Today many visitors who discover this property are not aware of its fascinating history.

Demolished in about 1834, King John's Tavern stood nearly opposite the narrow entrance to The Close, called Little Stile, in South Street. A magnificent example of pre-Tudor architecture, its history had been little documented. The interior was particularly notable and unique in the city. Such a building today would be greatly admired and valued. Its removal was the result of road widening. The projecting upper storey was supported by oak corbels carved with three figures. On the left of the door was a porter or door keeper who wielded a mace. The Royal coat of arms was above. On the right side of the door was a jester or fool with a cap and bells. Such images were often found in the houses of great nobles. The city coat of arms was shown above.

King John's Tavern contained a most impressive interior. Its most dominant feature was a massive oak winding staircase, above which was a vaulted plaster ceiling with rich mouldings. The Tudor Rose was an integral part of the design. Sumptuous pendants completed a masterpiece of decorative plasterwork. This view is from W. Cotton's *Elizabethan Guild*, which was published in 1873. The site was to become Lloyds cigarette factory.

The Devon and Exeter Hospital, which was opened in 1743, was the result of the initiative of Dean Alured Clarke. Land for the project was designated in Southernhay and given by the MP John Tuckfield. The building is shown in 1812 in a more rural setting than today. Opposite is the wall of Trinity Green burial ground, now the site of the Forte Crest Hotel car park.

This detail from Rocque's map of 1744 shows a view from the city wall to the Devon and Exeter Hospital. In the foreground, gardens extending to the city wall are being planted. The central walled area is Trinity Green burial ground, where a burial is taking place. The grave is dug and the body is being carried, covered with a cloth. A man with a large staff stands beside the grave. Other graves and tombstones are visible. To the right, a flock of sheep is dominated by a large ram. A simple hut is within the grounds. The hospital was not complete at this date but the artist has shown its proposed full size.

This vignette by Townsend, published by Besly, shows a view of Northernhay Gardens with some fine mature trees. On the right is Northernhay House, which has a double-gate entrance. This building stood in the grounds of Northernhay and was not part of the castle complex.

A view of Northernhay House. This is the only photographic record known to the author.

The Castle Hotel, Castle Street, 1937. The hotel stood at the junction of Old and New Castle Street. It was demolished to allow for the creation of Bailey Street after the war. A feature of the site were the massive wooden props used to shore up the adjacent building. Today the site has been built on.

The construction of a new police station in Waterbeer Street allowed the integration of Roman mosaics in the foyer floor. The incomplete mosaics were found close by during excavations. They were complemented by Victorian copies around the border. The floor was an item of some interest. After demolition of the police station, the floor was retained but ten years later it was destroyed after mistakenly being declared a fake!

The police station was opened in 1887 and demolished in the 1960s. Today only the foundation stone remains on the site. In front of the conical tower of the police station is the entrance to Pancras Lane, leading to Paul Street.

'The Vineyard', a large property, is situated on the south side of Exeter Castle. Its grounds are confined by the curtain wall of the castle and the city wall, and today it is known as Bradninch Hall. Bought by a syndicate in 1902, it was to become the Castle Street College Hostel for women students. This lithograph of 1859 by W. Spreat shows mature trees growing in the castle grounds.

Before the war, Dix's Field was one of the most elegant areas of the city. Two rows of terraces divided by a central garden provided fashionable accommodation and offices. These were built in 1805 by Matthew Nosworthy. Entry into 'the field' was past a bow-fronted Regency house, the birthplace of Revd Sabine Baring-Gould. He was born in 1834 and was the author of 'Onward Christian Soldiers'. In later years the house became a hotel, before being destroyed in 1942.

The Royal Public Rooms were built on the west side of the London Inn Square on the site of the old Bristol Inn. The famous Paganini, composer and violin virtuoso, had an apartment here while performing on his one-string violin. The Royal Public Rooms were opened in 1820 and paid for by the gentry. They were used for balls, concerts and general entertainment. After the Theatre Royal fire of 1887, the building became the Hippodrome Theatre and finally the Plaza Cinema. Northernhay Place is shown incomplete and coaches are offloading outside the New London Inn, a major coaching establishment. The Royal Public Rooms offered for hire a room of 100 ft x 36 ft and 40 ft in height, and a small room 56 ft x 19 ft 6 in. and 25 ft in height. The building, when it was the Plaza Cinema, was bombed in 1942, being engulfed by an enormous fire ball that destroyed it.

The advent of the Turnpike Act led to a major upgrading of Exeter's roads. In 1753, 477 people united to promote the scheme which involved nineteen roads radiating from the city. Many of these were ruinous and difficult to negotiate in the winter months. Repairs were to be paid for by collecting tolls. Each road had its own trustees and main roads had a toll house. At the expiration of the Turnpike Trust, all toll houses were sold. In a period of 130 years, phenomenal changes were to take place, allowing the greater movement of traffic around the region. These toll houses were drawn by George Townsend. Top, left to right: Stoke Hill, Red Cow. Middle: Mount Radford, Dunsford. Bottom: Blackboy.

This delightful drawing of the Elephant Inn with a pack horse is by Herbert Railton. The city has boasted a wealth of inns and taverns, but few records exist of these interesting properties. The large yard of the Elephant Inn accommodated horse-drawn vehicles. On the left is the rear of No. 38 North Street, a fourteenth-century building of great architectural interest, which was shamefully demolished for the rebuilding of the city centre.

Before the war, opposite St Stephen's Church in High Street, there was a narrow alley called Kings Alley. This led to the city baths, referred to as Kings Baths, which were blitzed in 1942. Kings Lodge is shown in about 1880, a substantial property built in 1734 by Richard King (owner or builder). Its site is where Musgrave House stands today. In 1829 it became a school and in 1887 baths were constructed in the grounds. In 1892 the YMCA took over the house, and in 1893 the city council stepped in to run the baths until their destruction in 1942.

The discovery of an ancient bath at the site of Barnfield Crescent during construction led to the architect's notion of building public baths. These were opened on 3 December 1821. Resembling a Grecian temple with a figure of Neptune flanked by a seahorse, a striking piece of classical architecture came into Southernhay. Three large porches, inscribed with 'Hot & Cold Baths' over the doorways, confronted clients. This facility was shortlived, being demolished in 1868 and replaced by a chapel.

In 1769 the first Exeter Bank was built by William Mackworth Praed in the Cathedral Close. This was followed by the building of the Royal Clarence Hotel (originally called, simply, the Hotel). It is seen here in about 1900, trading under the name Stanbury.

Taken from an old woodcut, this illustration shows the entry into Bedford Circus from High Street. The Devon and Exeter Bank had acquired a corner site and opened on 20 May 1839. The records of the City Council were kept in their fire-proof safe. The Bedford Chapel and the walled edge to the communal garden are visible.

Bedford Circus, which was built between 1773 and 1826 by the builders Robert Stribling and Giles Painter, offered the most prestigious accommodation. It was the finest example of Georgian architecture in the city and was of national importance. Although bomb damaged in 1942, Bedford Circus was not rebuilt.

Exeter's first theatre was built in Waterbeer Street. The second, shown here, was built in 1804 on the right after leaving Bedford Circus before entering Southernhay. This was burnt out in 1820, then rebuilt and burnt out again in 1885. In 1886 the Theatre Royal was constructed in Longbrook Street, but it too caught on fire in 1887, killing 186 people. It was demolished in 1963.

The New Western Market, or Lower Market, was designed by Charles Fowler and took two years to complete. The foundation stone was laid in 1835. The Italian-style building housed butchers, corn merchants, leather merchants, wool merchants, the Market House Inn and others. Entry from Fore Street was down a central avenue with shops on either side. The superstructure was supported by large granite columns with the Market Hall extending 157 ft x 91 ft. Although the structure still stood after being bombed in 1942, it was later demolished.

This charming painting shows the interior of the Lower Market being used as a soup kitchen. Iron racks for hanging carcasses are shown and, strangely, there is also a large cannon.

In 1850 a new Devon and Exeter Central School was built on a site overlooking Coombe Street in the West Quarter. Access was from Coombe Street or Rack Street. Hundreds of Exeter children were taught in this Victorian school before its demolition in 1978. This lithograph was produced to gain funds for its building.

A fine late sixteenth-century building stood in the north-east corner of The Close until it was destroyed in May 1942 by a direct hit from a high explosive bomb. Known as the 'Town House of the Abbots of Buckfastleigh', it had been in the ownership of numerous wealthy families. A splendid relief of Elizabeth I and a sundial embellished the front of the house. There was a large oval garden.

In 1632 the Mayor and Chamber converted part of St John's Hospital to a Free School. The building stood prominently in upper High Street (at the top of Princesshay), facing the street. To the left of the entrance was St John's Chapel and to the right was Exeter Free Grammar School. After 250 years the building was in a ruinous state and was removed. A new post office was built on the site in 1881 and was completed two years later.

The courtyard, 1845. After thirty-six years it was removed.

Left: This print of 1791 shows a building adjoining the Cathedral west front as a post office. Mr Jackson was the postmaster, and a woman and her two daughters delivered the mail. The office moved to Mrs Tredwins, Gandy Street, in 1850 to Queen Street, and finally to the corner of Northernhay Gardens and Queen Street. *Above*: Nos 83 and 84 Queen Street were opened as a post office in 1850. The classic façade with four massive Corinthian columns added a new dimension to the street, contrasting with the market opposite. The post office was run from this building for fourteen years. This illustration dates from 1840.

The old post office on the corner of Post Office Street, opposite Bampfylde House. The building contained one room manned by four people. This strange little building was one of seven properties that were used as post offices.

A replacement for the prison at South Gate was the House of Correction, built on the site of the Rougemont Hotel, Queen Street. Grossly overcrowded, it dealt with light sentences. However, children were regularly flogged and put to the treadmill. It was removed in 1863.

The Devon and Exeter Hotel Company purchased the site of the old prison in 1878 to construct a new Railway Hotel at a cost of £30,000. The railway came to Queen Street in 1860. This illustration shows the architect's conception of the finished building. The left wing and formal gardens did not transpire.

A meeting of the Exeter Chamber of Commerce resulted in the building of the Victoria Hall in Queen Street. It was completed for the visit of the British Association in 1869. The largest venue in Exeter, it could seat 1,500 people. On 6 October 1919 the hall caught fire and was gutted. Twenty-seven water jets were needed to quell the fire.

Numerous functions were held at the Victoria Hall, including in 1899 Harry Pole's Myriorama, a forerunner of the early cinema. Circuses also performed there regularly.

This remarkable complex of buildings extended from near the Cathedral west front to South Street. It was known as the College of the Vicars' Choral. Between 1850 and 1900, most buildings were removed. The hall survived, however, but was gutted in 1942; the ruins remain in South Street. This view is looking towards the Cathedral.

Erected under the instructions of Bishop Brantingham and completed in 1387, the College housed twenty-four singing cathedral priests in secure surroundings and within a short distance of the Cathedral. The complex also became known as Kalendarhay after Kalendar Brethren, who were earlier occupiers of the site. This painting is by Miss K.M. Clarke.

An intriguing picture of the hall in 1879, by Herbert Railton.

This excellent picture, painted by George Townsend (undated), shows Exeter Quay with the Ferryman's Cottage situated exactly opposite the landing-stage. The redevelopment of the quay cellars may have led to its removal and the ferryman moving to the cottage adjacent to Fountain Inn (now the Prospect).

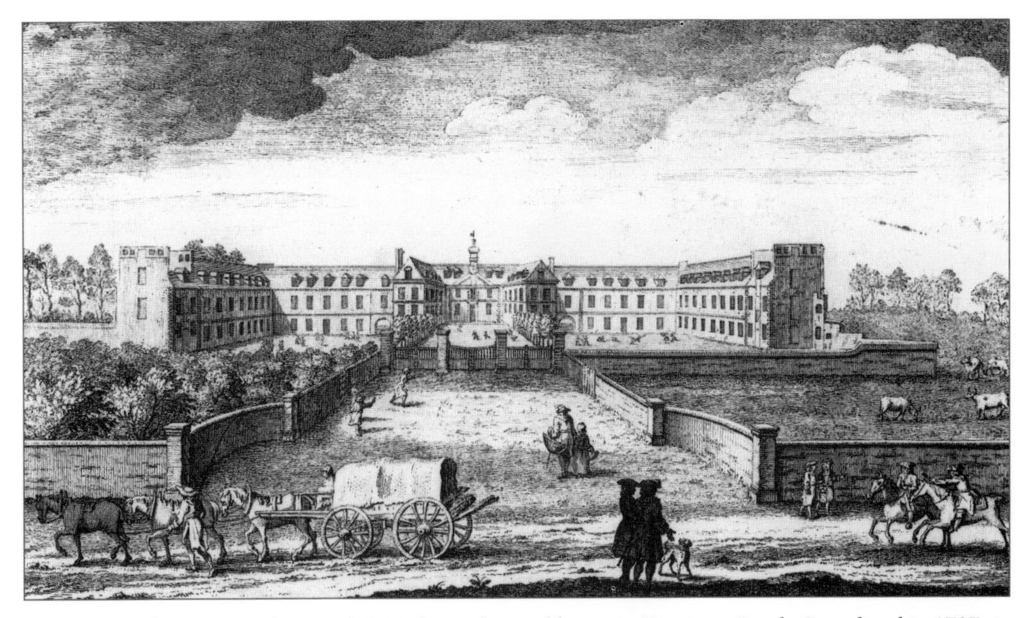

This vignette from Rocque's map of 1744 shows the workhouse in Heavitree Road. Completed in 1707, it resembled a French château. Catering for the poor of the city, it provided work in a brickfield and the gardens for the 234 inhabitants.

Mol's coffee house, dating from the sixteenth century, is one of Exeter's most famous properties. It is shown around 1820 with its original gable. This was replaced in 1868 by a new gable in Dutch style. The first-floor windows resemble those of a galleon. Traditionally the first-floor room was known as 'The Oak Room' because of its panelling. Forty-six coats of arms of famous Devon families decorate the panels. The Royal Coat of Arms of Elizabeth I was situated between the two bay windows until 1806, when it was replaced by a painted board of the original. The Cathedral Close is shown with a wooden rail, which was later replaced by railings

The destruction of many of Exeter's buildings is more than regrettable, being an indictment of attitudes towards the city's historical fabric. The utter destruction of No. 229 High Street was perhaps one of the worst examples. The Jacobean interior was ripped out and exported to America, being little valued in this country. It arrived in Kansas City, much to the joy of the museum and its visitors, where it was re-erected to show a classic interior of the period. This sad event occurred only sixty years ago.

Chapter Eight

The Cathedral and City Churches

The neo-classical St David's Church, built in 1816, was to find little favour with its congregation, with the result that it was demolished in 1897. Because of its design with a prominent rounded tower, it was referred to as the 'pepperpot' church. The character of the Victorian church that now occupies its site could not be more different.

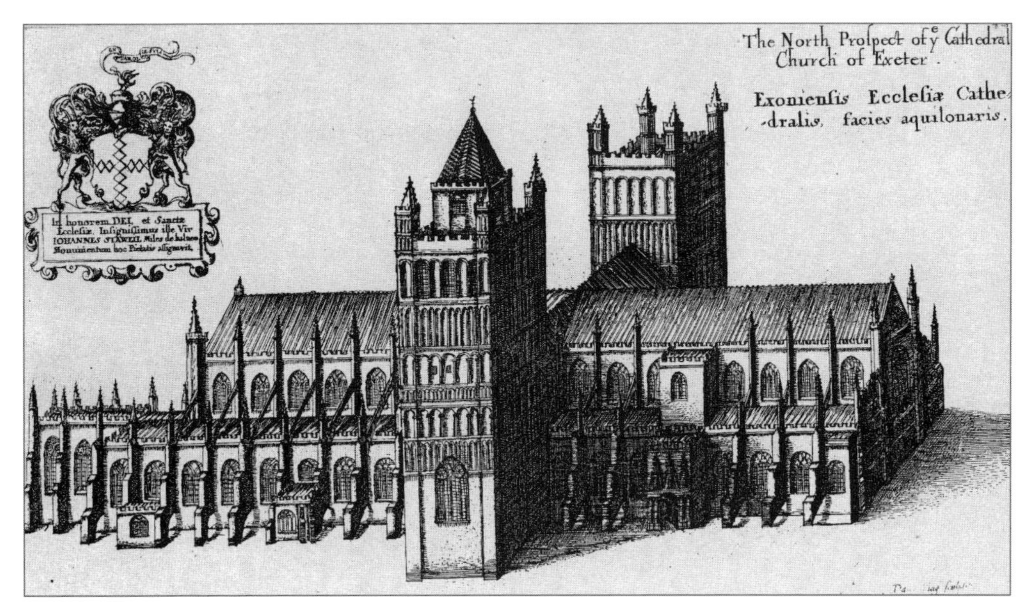

The earliest visual records of Exeter Cathedral, from 1650 to 1750, show a large wooden structure on the top of the north tower. It was capped by a spire and topped by a weather vane in the form of a cockerel. According to Mr Harry Hems, the well-known ecclesiastical sculptor, the arrival of the bell Great Peter in 1483 created a major problem, being too big to swing from within the north tower. The bell was therefore placed in a wooden structure on the roof of the tower. In 1484 the weathercock was fitted. It remained in position until 1752, and was then kept in the cathedral stores. In 1812 the Dean and Chapter presented the weathercock to St Sidwell's Church to be placed on its new spire. On 2 May 1900 the spire fell to the ground and was duly photographed by Hems' son. It was later regilded by the ex-warden and replaced on 10 May 1910. At that time the weathercock was 417 years old. The church was bombed in 1942, destroying a unique relic.

The Crowing Cock, photographed by H. Turner Hems, was said to be the oldest representation of a crowing cock utilized as a vane existing in the whole world, according to Harry Hems. It measured 2 ft 9 in from the point of the beak to the extreme curve of the outside tail and was 2 ft 6 in high.

Rocque's map of 1744 gives a fascinating insight into the Cathedral Close. At this time it was a meeting-place for gentlemen in business. An enclosure with two large wooden gates is visible with two wigged men in discussion. Around a hundred trees were cut from Duryard Wood to rail in The Close, and rows of elm trees were planted. An inn with a balcony is on the right. At the end of the walkway across The Close is the early St Mary Major Church and the entrance to the College of the Vicars Choral. The cathedral weathercock is also visible and the treasurer's house abuts the north tower.

'The West Prospect of The Close', also from Rocque's map, shows to the right St Mary Major Church with dwellings built against the tower. In 1800 it was recorded that 108 houses inhabited by 114 families, amounting to 571 people, occupied The Close of St Peter's Church.

This view of 1791 shows the erection of railings on the west front of the Cathedral. At this time wooden railings still existed in The Close. On the right is the entrance to the College of the Vicars Choral. The perspective is somewhat suspect.

Exeter Cathedral, *c.* 1830, showing the introduction of iron railings around The Close. A water pump had been introduced outside the west front at the end of the wooden railings. A fine gas street lamp also indicates the beginning of a new era in the Cathedral Close.

To stand at the West Door of Exeter Cathedral and look down the nave is an awesome sight. Thirty Purbeck columns support the massive Gothic fan-vaulted roof. The size and space of the interior of the nave were one of its greatest assets until twentieth-century clutter encroached upon the space, and the interior subsequently lost some of its dynamic simplicity. This fine architectural perspective of the mid-eighteenth century shows the nave before the removal of the high box pews and pulpit.

Today the Cathedral chapter house is used for many purposes and its appearance has changed since these two photographs were taken. Here it is set out as the library, with bookcases and open shelves used to store hundreds of books. Today the library is situated in the Bishop's Palace.

The chapter house, showing the east window (1458 to 1465) by Bishop Nevylle. The later Victorian Gothic fireplace was removed.

The Cathedral west front, *c.* 1920. The building is enclosed by mature elm trees and St Mary Major Church; both buildings are blackened and dirty. General pollution, the elements and war had all taken their toll, together with the tradition of lighting bonfires outside the west front. The Cathedral has been the subject of a considerable ongoing restoration programme.

This small steel engraving shows a view looking from Broadgate to St Mary Major Church. It was said that this church could be traced back to Saxon times. Like many buildings, it was to receive additions and alterations. The church was removed in 1865.

The construction of a church so close to the Cathedral often caused comment, but on this site were found the possible remains of the city's first church, which pre-dated the Cathedral, during excavations. The site can therefore be classified as probably the most historic, as here too lie the remains of the Roman legionary bath house, one of the most important finds in the country.

In 1865 the new Victorian Church of St Mary Major was built on the site of the old church. Ironically, it was to last only 105 years before its demolition owing to lack of use. This record shows the church when it was first illuminated.

The interior of St Mary Major Church.

This photograph, taken by the author in 1965, shows St Mary Major Church before its demolition.

The tiny church of St Pancras narrowly missed destruction with the rebuilding of the city centre in the 1970s. The retention of this thirteenth-century church led to it being surrounded by alien architecture in the Guildhall Shopping Centre. Its interior was unsympathetically altered, giving little consideration to the antiquity of the building. St Pancras' Church was in a dilapidated state in the early nineteenth century, restored in 1831 and again in 1888. The pulpit came from Allhallows Church in Goldsmith Street. Its handrail is on the left.

The very early Saxon church of St George was found in South Street opposite Little Style, a narrow entrance to the Cathedral Close. It was demolished in 1843 to allow for road widening. An enclosed, railed site was left, which in 1942 was bombed, exposing the remains of the Saxon doorway. After the war this was placed in the ruin of the hall of the College of the Vicars Choral, where it can still be seen.

The Mint Wesleyan Chapel set back at the top of Fore Street had its own burial ground. The chapel, which opened in 1813, stood on the site of an Arian meeting-house. The burial ground was retained until 1867. Some tombstones still remain on the site.

The interior of The Mint Chapel, Fore Street, designed by Methodist architect William Jenkins and built by John Brown.

St Mary Arches Church is today a Christian Resources Centre. This pre-war photograph shows the unaltered interior with its simple Norman arches, from which the church derives its name. Used as the civic church, its roof was unfortunately destroyed in the Second World War. It was to be reconstructed using timbers from a wooden barge at Topsham.

St John's Church, dating from the early eleventh century, had a varied history. The building shown here is possibly fifteenth century, but has been subject to a number of alterations. Made in Heavitree sandstone, it was a dominant building in Fore Street. The body of the church was removed in 1937 but the tower remained. The clock was removed from the tower in 1938 because of its weight, then finally the tower was taken down in 1957.

St John's Bow led from Fore Street to Smythen Street, but was declared structurally unsound in 1843 and thus removed.

Changes to the street level in Fore Street in 1770 required alterations to St John's Church. The result was that the parishioners had to ascend stairs immediately on entering the building. A simple gallery was a feature of the interior.

Bartholomew Yard, a burial ground since 1637, was to be the site for a Victorian church built in 1843. Its name, Allhallows, was taken from an earlier church, Allhallows on the Wall, which stood on the city wall in Fore Street. The church was removed to allow the breaching of the wall for the construction of New Bridge Street, a continuation of Fore Street, in 1770.

The Victorian church of Allhallows was not well patronized. In 1938, after ninety-five years, the church fittings and furniture were removed, the building being demolished in 1950. The interior is shown prior to 1938.

Allhallows' Church was used for other purposes before its demolition. This included a corset factory and as a place for making parachutes for the war effort.

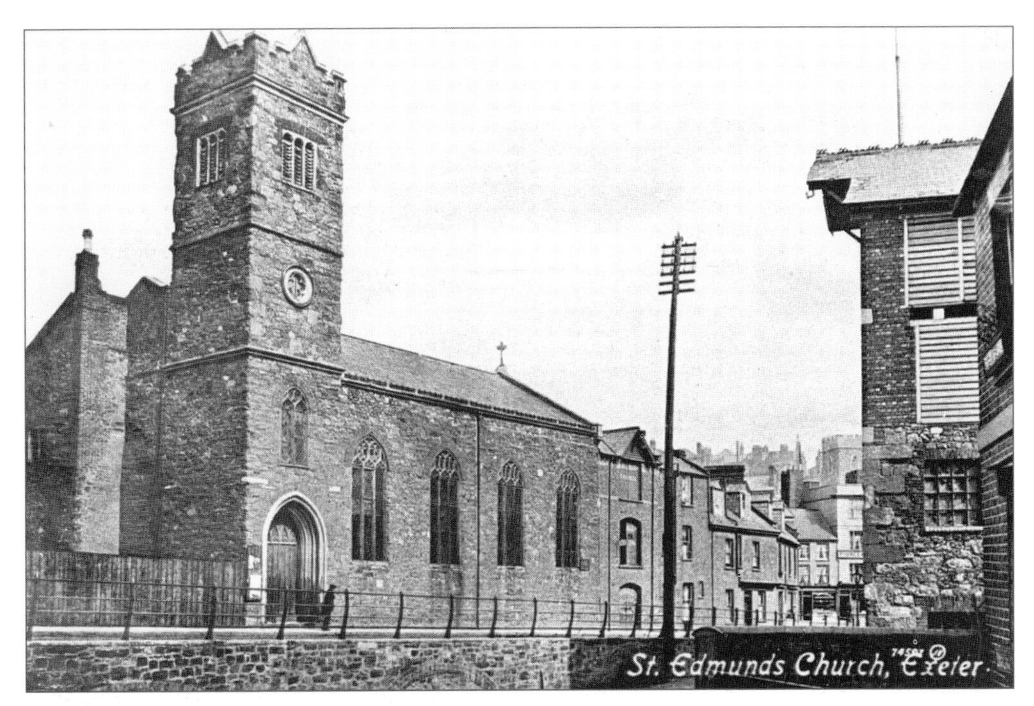

A rare feature of Exeter's medieval bridge was the church of St Edmund, which was built in conjunction with it. It is a feature of the earliest maps. This church dates from 1833 and was mostly demolished in the 1970s. The arches of the old bridge can just be seen. Today the ruins still stand and the remains of the bridge are exposed.

This engraving shows the thirteenth-century church of St Edmund on the Bridge. By 1800 the building was exhibiting signs of wear, but in 1832 it was burnt down, its replacement being built the following year.

Paul Street was at one time a 'living' back street. It took its name from the church on the corner of Goldsmith Street and Paul Street. The church, built in 1860 according to an Italian design, was a replacement for a much earlier building. The decline of the congregation led to the demolition of the church in 1936.

One of the city's earliest photographic records is that of the laying of the foundation stone of Southernhay Congregational Church in 1868. In the background is the site of the demolished bath house, which was replaced by a chapel.

This view of Southernhay on the south side is looking towards the Southernhay Congregational Church. The entrance to Dix's Field is behind the church.

In 1942, St Sidwell's Church was badly bombed, its tower being cut in half and the building gutted. The fifteenth-century church had been restored in the nineteenth century. In 1812 a new spire was added, topped by the weathercock from the Cathedral.

St Stephen's Church, High Street, with its original railings. Dating from 1664, the building stands on the foundation of an earlier church, recorded in the eleventh century. A sealed crypt still exists. A sign on the lamppost reads: 'Public Swimming Baths' and 'Hot and Cold Baths'. On the church wall a notice states: 'City of Exeter, YMCA Exactly opposite (up alley) ie Kings Alley'.

In 1905 the church of St Petrock, High Street, was exposed after years of being hidden from view. Buildings at the South Street end of High Street were swept away to allow street widening, in preparation for the introduction of the new electric trams. At this time the City Bank had yet to be completed (left).

The fifteenth-century Elyot window, now integrated into the Bishop's Palace, is seen here in its original position. The window formed part of the property adjacent to St Petrock's Church in the Cathedral Close and for some time was obscured from view. This watercolour indicates that it was found at the rear of Passmores and Saverys.

The most famous feature on St Lawrence's Church, High Street, was the statue of Elizabeth I, which was positioned in an alcove over the doorway. The porch had been constructed from the remnants of the conduit in High Street in 1694. The statue had also stood on the conduit. The fifteenth-century church was blitzed in 1942 and the remains demolished. The statue survives and can be seen in Exeter's Underground Passages Interpretation Centre. The church of St Lawrence is recorded as far back as 1222. Today the Cooperative Bank occupies the site.

Adjacent to St Lawrence's Church was a small passageway that led to its cemetery at the rear of the building. The entrance is under the shop sign, 'Shoe Co'. A small iron gate closed the passage. Excavations after the Second World War uncovered tombstones bearing the opening date of the burial ground: 1692.

An integral part of the design for Bedford Circus was the building of a chapel on the west side. This was consecrated in 1833 and was a popular venue. This fine building was blitzed in 1942 and its shell demolished.

In 1962 the classical fronted Christ Church in Southernhay, built in 1847, was demolished. The replacement office block is lacking in sympathy for its fine surroundings. Such areas as Southernhay are of historical and architectural interest. It is sad to see buildings erected in such areas which have little architectural merit when high-quality modern designs can complement rather than clash.

This rare photograph shows St David's Church before its demolition in 1897.

The diminutive church of Allhallows, dating from the twelfth century, occupied the corner site of Goldsmith Street and High Street and was demolished to allow for street widening and greater traffic access. Strangely, the little church was enclosed by other buildings in 1618 and at a later date a shop was constructed against its south wall. These were removed in 1880 and the church demolished in 1906.

The interior of Allhallows' Church, Goldsmith Street, the first church in Exeter to be lit by gas.

Allhallows' Church after the removal of the seventeenth-century buildings. The later shopfront was retained at this point and the walls rendered.

In the nineteenth century, Allhallows was subject to periods of restoration, specifically in 1883. Twenty-three years later the building was demolished. The shopfront is shown removed with the rendering having been taken off the walls. The west wall had been rebuilt and a new window inserted.

St Martin's Church is mainly fifteenth century with seventeenth- and eighteenth-century additions and furnishings. It was, however, consecrated in 1065. Catherine Street has a new building, introducing an unsuitable style for this ancient thoroughfare. This photograph was taken in about 1930.

CHAPTER NINE

FINAL DETAILS

CHIMNEY-PIECES

Chimney-piece found in the dining-room of No. 171 Fore Street.

Office in Gandy Street.

Chimney-piece from Bampfylde House, moved to Poltimore House.

Office in Gandy Street.

Chimney-piece from Stead and Simpson, Parliament Street. In 1913 part of a Tudor room was discovered containing the fireplace and part of an oak-framed window. This can still be seen in Samuel's, the jewellers, in Trichay Street.

Chimney-piece from the Civet Cat Public House, High Street.

Chimney-piece from Merlin Fryer, solicitor, Gandy Street.

Visitors to the Royal Albert Memorial Museum who view the newly refurbished local history gallery will have the opportunity to see a splendid medieval fireplace, which is a focal point in the new display. This impressive piece of medieval craftsmanship has only recently been highlighted as one of the city's important historical objects. Commissioned by the Precentor, John Coombe (1496–9), the fireplace was sculpted in Beer stone and placed in the chantry in the Cathedral Close. The building was demolished in 1870 and the only artefact to survive was the fireplace. Stored for thirty years, it was then installed in the Deanery where it remained until 1972. The Church authorities may have been under the impression that it was a Victorian replica. It was obtained by the museum and authenticated as being the original fireplace. This unique photograph shows the John Coombe fireplace in its original setting in the chantry, and it appears to have been taken just before the removal of the fireplace in 1870. The Cathedral School now occupies the site of the chantry.

EXETER'S DOORS

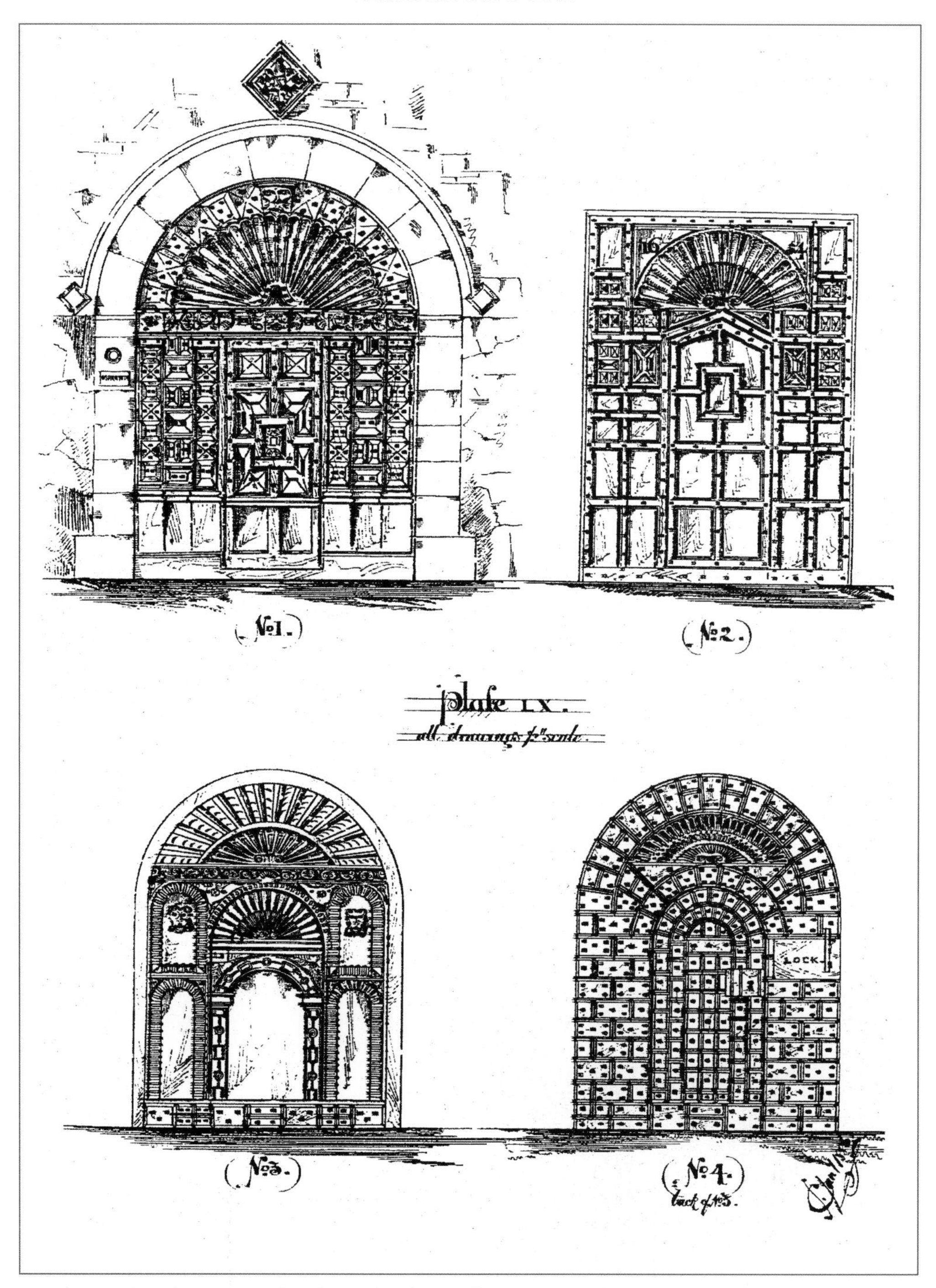

1 The Quadrangle, No. 10 The Close. This door still exists.
2 Morgans Court, Sidwell Street, 1654.
3 The front view of the Guildhall, still existing.
4 Guildhall, rear view.

The Globe Hotel, South Street.

The entrance to St John's Hospital, with blue boy statues, 1861. (The statues originally stood in the playground.)

DECORATIVE PLASTER CEILINGS

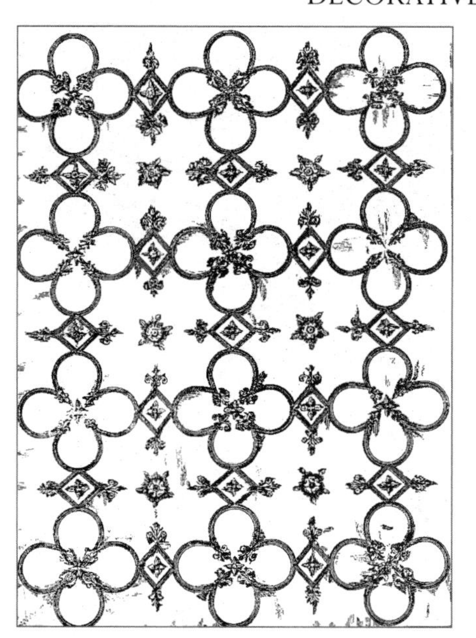

St Nicholas' Priory.

No. 171 Fore Street.

No. 80 Fore Street.

Bampfylde House.

The Apollo ceiling *in situ*. Nos 25 and 26 High Street, formerly the New Inn, contained this remarkable decorated plaster ceiling. It was probably the finest example in the city. The last owners of the property encouraged visitors to view it, and the ceiling formed part of one of their most prominent showrooms. The property was bombed in 1942 and the ceiling lost.

The interior of the Chevalier Inn, Fore Street.

FOUNTAINS

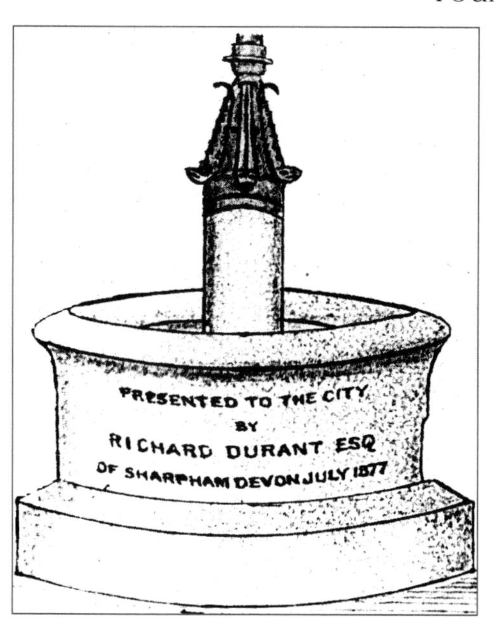

A fountain at the junction of Holloway Street, South Street and Magdalen Road.

A fountain in the castle yard.

The conduit, Milk Street, erected in 1838. This existed until shortly after the Second World War, when it was demolished.

AWNING SUPPORT

Exeter shop blinds were supported by decorative brass poles, which were inserted into metal fittings in kerb stones. These fittings can still be seen in Exeter streets.

LAMP STANDARDS

Lamp standards at the entrance to Dix's Field.

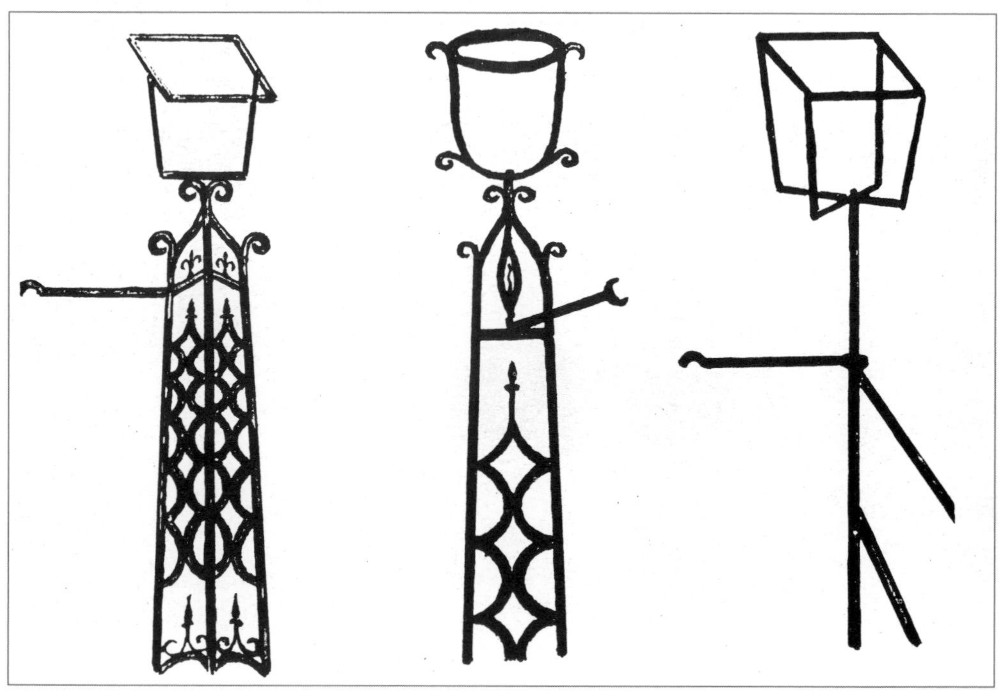

Oil lamp standards, Southernhay Green.

CLOCKS

The famous Bruford's clock, carved by Harry Hems, was held up by a figure of Old Father Time. Upright, the figure would have reached 10 ft in height. The clock with its famous support was destroyed in the blitz of 1942.

THE STATUE OF ST PETER

A reproduction of an early undated drawing of the figure of St Peter in its first position, supporting a building on the corner of North Street (see text p. 160).

One of Exeter's most intriguing antiquities is the statue of St Peter, which is said to have stood on the corner of High Street and North Street for 400 years or more. The oak figure has always been a subject for speculation – who put it there and why? The almost life-size

The corner of North Street and High Street, *c.* 1890, showing the statue in position, facing towards Fore Street.

A detailed photograph of the statue of St Peter, probably taken after its restoration in 1930.

figure is a detailed piece of early craftsmanship adorned in bright colours. It is possibly fifteenth or sixteenth century. St Peter holds a church and keys in one hand and a bible in the other. His foot stands on a figure, which it has been suggested represents paganism.

Early photographs prove the statue's existence in two positions on the site and a watercolour may prove a third. Latterly, St Peter stood in an alcove overlooking the High Street, but it was recently removed for restoration and is now on display in the Royal Albert Memorial Museum local history gallery. The corner site now remains without a statue for the first time in several hundred years.

Jenkins, the historian, says in his book of 1806 that this statue was in fact a support for a corner building. In 1738 Andrew Brice, an Exeter publisher, wrote the following verse:

> By this where houses, whelving houses meet, and vault, with beetle brows,
> a shelving street.
> Where stout St Peter on the corner stall props the impending edifice from
> fall.

St Peter's statue in its third position overlooking High Street, after the rebuilding of the corner of the street, which was occupied by J. Hepworth & Son. The company gave the statue to the city as a public memorial.

A previously undiscovered drawing, published here for the first time (see p. 158), shows the very early house in question, supported by the figure at ground-floor level. The building, very likely dating from the fifteenth or sixteenth century, has a most unusual castellated design on the upper storey; the owner was probably someone of considerable wealth.

Could there have been some religious significance to the siting of the figure of St Peter? Perhaps it was placed there so that it could be touched by pilgrims or others making their way to the Cathedral from the west. Perhaps it was originally positioned in the Cathedral itself, before being integrated into the building. These questions will probably never be answered, but the ancient drawing increases our understanding of the background to the figure.

In 1930 the City Council accepted the statue from J. Hepworth & Son, who had restored it. Kept in its position overlooking High Street, it was declared a public memorial for all to see and today remains under the Council's care.